Summary of

Thinking, Fast and Slow

by Daniel Kahneman

Instaread

Instaread on Thinking, Fast and Slow by Daniel Kahneman

Please Note

This is an unofficial summary.

Copyright © 2014 by InstaRead Summaries. All rights reserved worldwide. No part of this publication may be reproduced or transmitted in any form without the prior written consent of the publisher.

Limit of Liability/Disclaimer of Warranty: The publisher and author make no representations or warranties with respect to the accuracy or completeness of these contents and disclaim all warranties such as warranties of fitness for a particular purpose. The author or publisher are not liable for any damages whatsoever. The fact that an individual or organization is referred to in this document as a citation or source of information does not imply that the author or publisher endorses the information that the individual or organization provided. This concise summary is unofficial and is not authorized, approved, licensed, or endorsed by the original book's author or publisher.

Table of Contents

Overview 5
Important People 8
Introduction 11
Chapter Summaries and Key Takeaways 13
Part 1 13
Chapter 1 13
Chapter 2 16
Chapter 3 18
Chapter 4 20
Chapter 5 22
Chapter 6 24
Chapter 7 25
Chapter 8 27
Chapter 9 29
Part 2 30
Chapter 10 30
Chapter 11 31
Chapter 12 32
Chapter 13 33
Chapter 14 34
Chapter 15 35
Chapter 16 37
Chapter 17 39
Chapter 18 40

Instaread on Thinking, Fast and Slow by Daniel Kahneman

Part 3 41
Chapter 19 41
Chapter 20 43
Chapter 21 44
Chapter 22 45
Chapter 23 46
Chapter 24 47
Part 4 48
Chapter 25 48
Chapter 26 49
Chapter 27 50
Chapter 28 51
Chapter 29 52
Chapter 30 54
Chapter 31 55
Chapter 32 56
Chapter 33 58
Chapter 34 59
Part 5 60
Chapter 35 60
Chapter 36 61
Chapter 37 62
Chapter 38 63
Conclusions 64
A Reader's Perspective 65

Overview

Daniel Kahneman, author of the book *Thinking, Fast and Slow*, sets out to create a new vocabulary of words and definitions to describe mental errors. He hopes that readers will recognize these errors in others and in themselves and learn how to correct them.

System 1 is described as a fictional character representing the intuitive process of the brain and System 2 is described as a fictional character representing the deliberate thinking process of the brain. The two systems have different roles but work together to assess our world and guide us in our decision-making.

Kahneman makes the case that too often we suffer mental fallacies because we are too quick to accept the information that the automatic System 1 provides for us without first carefully analyzing it with our System 2 process. He claims that the brain in its attempt to be efficient takes shortcuts which cause us to have errors in judgment. This shows that our brains are inherently lazy.

The intuitive side of our brain attempts to create a story or narrative of our lives from the information it receives.

Instaread on Thinking, Fast and Slow by Daniel Kahneman

This information is limited to our own experience so we do not always have the whole picture. This results in errors of substitution, stereotyping, **WYSIATI** (what you see is all there is), causal explanations, base-rate neglect, the halo effect, the framing effect, the anchoring effect, narrative fallacy, illusion of validity, illusion of skill, and overconfidence in what we think we know. Kahneman defines these terms in an attempt to give people a new way of talking about mental fallacies.

Kahneman compares those who live in the land of theory with those who act in the real world. Basically, he is comparing the way economists look at people as opposed to how psychologists look at people. Those in the land of economic theory he calls the Econs, while those who act in the real world are the Humans. Econs are always logical and rational while Humans cannot help but be illogical and irrational because their thinking is flawed. They ignore statistical information and lead their lives based on causal connections and explanations. Theoretically, Econs tend to see things as black or white with no choice in-between. In reality, Humans are not Econs and see a range of options before them.

Lastly, Kahneman compares the experiencing self and the remembering self. The experiencing self does the living while the remembering self keeps score and makes choices. The experiencing-self answers the question, "How are things right now?" The remembering-self answers the question, "How was it, on the whole?" Our brains confuse the actual experience with the memory of the experience.

In the final chapters of the book, Kahneman talks about how we experience happiness and well-being. Because humans focus their attention on select moments and neglect what happens at other times, they have a distorted view of what happiness really is. Kahneman states "the word *happiness* does not have a simple meaning and should not be used as if it does." (p. 308). He describes well-being as what occurs when people's lives are filled with experiences they would rather continue than stop. Resistance to interruption is a sign that someone is experiencing well-being. According to Kahneman, the easiest way for people to increase happiness is to control their use of time. Finding more time to do the things they really enjoy will increase their happiness level. Affective forecasting, the focusing illusion, and the passing of time all influence how satisfied people are with their lives. The reference points they compare their lives to also contribute to how much happiness they actually experience.

Important People

System 1: System 1 is a fictional representation of the automatic and intuitive process of the brain.

System 2: System 2 is a fictional representation of the process of the brain that requires effort and attention.

Daniel Kahneman: Kahneman is the author of the book, *Thinking, Fast and Slow*. He is a psychologist and professor who has done extensive research in the field of judgment and decision-making.

Amos Tvresky: Tversky was the research partner of Daniel Kahneman. He was an expert in the field of decision research. The two first met when Kahneman invited Tversky to be a guest speaker for a seminar that he was teaching.

Mihaly Csikszentmihalyi: Some people experience a state of mind of effortless concentration so deep that they lose their sense of time, of themselves, and of their problems. Csikszentmihalyi is the psychologist who dubbed this state of mind, "flow."

Walter Mischel: Mischel is a psychologist who conducted experiments with four-year-old children to examine the connection between thinking and self-control.

Shane Frederick: Frederick constructed the Cognitive Reflection Test which was comprised of questions and puzzles. This test showed that individuals who followed their intuitions without question were more impulsive and more impatient.

Sarnoff Mednick: Mednick is the psychologist who defined the essence of creativity as associative memory that works very well.

Alex Todorov: Todorov illustrated that people have the ability to evaluate the shape of a stranger's face to determine how dominant he is and how trustworthy he is.

Paul Slovic: Slovic is a psychologist who has proposed that people let their likes and dislikes determine their beliefs about the world without really seeking out the truth.

Norbert Schwarz: Schwarz is a psychologist who studied the availability heuristic. The availability heuristic occurs when the mind bases its judgment on the probability of an event happening. The probability is determined by the number of similar incidences it has stored in memory and how easy it is for the brain to recall those incidences.

Nassim Taleb: Taleb, a psychologist and statistician, introduced the idea of a narrative fallacy which describes how flawed stories of the past shape our views of the world and our expectations for the future.

Paul Meehl: Meehl revealed 20 studies that proved that the accuracy of experts was matched or exceeded by a simple algorithm. In these studies, clinical predictions based on the impressions of trained professionals were compared to statistical predictions made by combining scores or ratings according to a rule. The statistical predictions were as accurate or more so than those of the experts.

Herbert Simon: Simon was a scholar and researcher with many titles to his name: political scientist, economist, sociologist, psychologist, and professor. He defined intuition as "nothing more and nothing less than recognition."

Daniel Bernoulli: Bernoulli was a Swiss mathematician and physicist who observed that most people dislike risk, and if they are offered a choice between a gamble and an amount equal to its expected value, they will choose the sure thing.

Introduction

In this book Daniel Kahneman hopes to identify and understand errors of judgment and choice. He wants to provide a richer and more accurate vocabulary to discuss these errors. He worked with his colleague, Amos Tversky, doing research on intuitive statistics. The two of them had already concluded in an earlier seminar that their own intuitions were lacking. Their subjective judgments were biased, they were too willing to believe research findings based on inadequate evidence, and they collected too few observations in their own research. The goal of their study was to find out whether other researchers had this problem as well.

Kahneman and Tversky found that participants in their studies ignored the relevant statistical facts and relied exclusively on resemblance. They used resemblance as a heuristic (rule of thumb) to simplify things when making a difficult judgment. Relying on this heuristic caused predictable biases (systematic errors) in their predictions. The research partners learned that people tend to determine the importance of issues by how easy they are retrieved from their memory. This is brought about in large part by the extent of coverage of the issues in the media.

Kahneman presents a view of how the mind works, drawing on recent developments in cognitive and social psychology. He explains the differences between fast (intuitive) thinking and slow (deliberate) thinking. People have a limitation in their minds: an excessive confidence in what they think they know.

Instaread on Thinking, Fast and Slow by Daniel Kahneman

Thank you for purchasing this Instaread book

**Download the Instaread mobile app to get
unlimited text & audio summaries
of bestselling books.**

Visit Instaread.co
to learn more.

Chapter Summaries and Key Takeaways

Part 1

Chapter 1

The difference between looking at a photograph of a person and looking at a math problem illustrates two types of thinking. Looking at a photograph of a person illustrates intuitive or fast thinking. Impressions of what is happening in the photograph come to mind automatically and effortlessly. The brain instantly determines details such as the person's mood or the color of a person's hair. Looking at a math problem illustrates deliberate or slow thinking. The process of slow thinking is mental work involving effort. Slow thinking also involves the body. Solving a math problem causes a person's muscles to tense up, blood pressure to rise, and heart rate to increase.

The terms "System 1" and "System 2" for the two systems of the mind are the fictional characters of this book.

Instaread on Thinking, Fast and Slow by Daniel Kahneman

System 1 operates automatically while System 2 requires effort. System 1 operations can generate complex patterns of ideas, but only System 2 can construct thoughts in an orderly series of steps. The two systems each have their own individual abilities, limitations, and functions.

System 1 includes innate skills that we were born with and other activities that have become automatic through prolonged practice. Some of these skills are completely involuntary, while others, such as chewing, can be controlled voluntarily but normally are automatic.

System 2 operations require attention and are disrupted when attention is drawn away. System 2 activities require effort. It is difficult or impossible to conduct several at once. Intense focusing on a certain task can make people blind to other things.

The two systems interact with each other in various ways. When System 1 encounters difficulty, it calls on System 2 for more details to solve the problem at hand. System 2 is also credited with self-control. The two systems divide labor to minimize effort and optimize performance. This works well most of the time, but System 1 sometimes has biases. These biases are systematic errors made under certain circumstances. Additionally, System 1 cannot be turned off.

Key Takeaways

- There are two main processes of the brain labeled as the fictitious characters, System 1 and System 2. Each has its own attributes and characteristics.

- System 1 skills are intuitive and automatic, while System 2 skills require attention and effort.

Chapter 2

The thoughts and actions of System 2 are often guided by the intuitions and impulses of System 1. However, there are vital tasks that only System 2 can perform because they require effort and acts of self-control.

Studies have shown the pupils of the eyes are good indicators of mental effort. They dilate substantially when people are working and stop dilating or shrink when they stop working.

The designation of attention from the brain has been determined by evolutionary history. Responding quickly to threats or to promising opportunities improves the chance of survival. As a result, System 1 takes over in emergencies and gives priority to self-protective actions.

The "law of least effort" applies to both cognitive and physical exertion. This law maintains that if there are several ways to reach the same goal, people will eventually go to the least-demanding course of action. The brain seeks out ways to be more efficient. Laziness is built into our nature. An important discovery of cognitive psychologists is that switching from one task to another requires a lot of effort, especially when under the pressure of time limits. People normally avoid mental overload by dividing tasks into multiple, easy steps.

System 2 can follow rules, compare objects, and make deliberate choices. System 1 is not capable of these tasks. System 2 also has the vital capability of programming memory to follow an instruction that overrides habitual responses.

Key Takeaways

- System 1 and System 2 work together to accomplish goals.

- The brain is constantly seeking ways to make sense of the world and to be more efficient.

- Law of least effort applies to both cognitive and physical exertion. Laziness is built into our nature.

Chapter 3

It is usually easy to walk and think at the same time, but these activities, when at their extremes, compete for the limited resources of System 2. If someone, who is walking at a comfortable speed, is asked to do a complicated math problem, that person will most likely stop in his tracks. A faster walk brings about a sharp deterioration in the ability to think coherently. These examples show that physical activity and deliberate thought draw on the same limited budget of effort. They also show that maintaining a coherent train of thought requires discipline.

Cognitive work is not always unpleasant. Some people experience a state of effortless concentration so deep that they lose their sense of time, of themselves, and of their problems. This state of mind was named "flow" by psychologist Mihaly Csikszentmihalyi. It brings about a state of joy and is known as an optimal experience.

It has been proven that both self-control and cognitive effort are forms of mental work. Studies have shown that people who are simultaneously challenged by a difficult cognitive task and by a temptation are more likely to yield to the temptation. In other words, System 1 has more influence on behavior when System 2 is busy. In addition to cognitive load, alcohol use and insufficient sleep can cause weakened self-control. Self-control requires attention and effort which means it is a task performed by System 2.

One of the main jobs of System 2 is to monitor and control actions that are suggested by System 1. System

2 allows some of these actions but suppresses or modifies others. Many people are overconfident and place too much faith in their intuitions. When people believe something is true, they are more likely to believe arguments that support it, even when these arguments are unsound. The involvement of System 1 makes the conclusion come first and the arguments follow. Intelligence is not just the ability to reason. It is also the ability to find relevant information in memory and to pay attention when it is needed.

Key Takeaways

- Self-control and deliberate thought are both forms of mental work.

- Some people can experience a mental state of "flow." This is a state of joy and is considered an optimal experience.

Chapter 4

Associative activation is a process in which ideas, that have been evoked, trigger many other ideas in a spreading cascade of activity in the brain. These elements are all connected, and they support and strengthen each other. When someone reads two words that are oddly juxtaposed, System 1 makes as much sense from them as possible. The body, as well as the brain, reacts to this juxtaposition of words with an emotional and a physical response. Cognitive scientists have recognized in recent years that people think with their body, not just their brain.

Scientists have discovered that exposure to a word makes it easier for related words to be evoked. This is called a priming effect. In addition, the primed words have some ability to prime other ideas. Priming is not limited to words and concepts. Action and emotions can also be primed. This priming phenomenon, the influencing of an action by an idea, is known as the ideomotor effect. Reciprocal links are common in the association of ideas and actions. For example, being amused makes you smile and smiling makes you feel amused. When people first learn about priming, their reaction is often disbelief. This is because System 2 believes that it is in charge and knows the reasons for its choices. Priming occurs in System 1 and people have no conscious access to it.

Key Takeaways

- Associative activation is a process of the brain in which ideas trigger other ideas.

- The priming effect occurs when exposure to a word makes it easier for related words to be evoked. Actions and emotions can also be primed and form reciprocal links to each other.

Instaread on Thinking, Fast and Slow by Daniel Kahneman

Chapter 5

Whenever a person is conscious, multiple assessments are carried out by System 1. One of the assessments is for cognitive ease. When someone is in a state of cognitive ease, he is probably in a good mood, likes what he sees, believes what he hears, trusts his intuitions, and feels that his situation is comfortably familiar. When feeling cognitively strained, a person is more likely to be vigilant and suspicious, invest more effort in what he is doing, feel less comfortable, and make fewer errors. A cognitively strained person is also less intuitive and less creative.

Memory is susceptible to illusion. Words that have been seen before are easier to see again. This is known as the illusion of familiarity. The impression of familiarity is produced by System 1, and System 2 relies on that impression.

When writing a persuasive letter, anything that can be done to reduce cognitive strain will help increase credibility. Ways to do this include: maximizing legibility, making the message simple, making the message memorable, choosing names that are easy to pronounce, and putting ideas into verse, if possible. Cognitive ease is associated with good feelings, which will make people more receptive to the intuitions of System 1.

Key Takeaways

- When a person is in cognitive ease, he is generally in a good mood, feels comfortable, believes what he hears and is relaxed.

- When a person is in cognitive strain, he is feeling vigilant and suspicious. He puts more effort into what he is doing.

Chapter 6

System 1's main function is assessing what is normal in each person's world. Having the capacity for surprise is an important part of our mental life. There are two main types of surprise. First, a person is surprised when an actively expected event does not occur. Second, a person is surprised when something unexpected happens. When this second type happens, a reoccurrence of this event is less surprising. In this way, abnormal events begin to appear normal. Studies of brain responses have shown that violations of normality are detected very quickly. Finding causal connections in a story is an automatic process of System 1. When presented with a surprise, System 1 works to make connections to create a coherent interpretation of the surprise.

Key Takeaway

- The main function of System 1 is to determine what is normal in a person's world. It works to make connections to create a coherent interpretation of each situation.

Chapter 7

System 1 functions mainly by jumping to conclusions. This becomes risky when a situation is unfamiliar, the stakes are high, and there is no time to collect more information. These circumstances make intuitive errors probable. Basically, System 1 bets on an answer based on experience. Recent events and current context carry the most weight in determining an interpretation. System 1 is biased to believe certain things, and System 2 is in charge of doubting and unbelieving. System 2, however, is sometimes busy and often lazy. When System 2 is otherwise engaged, a person will believe almost anything that System 1 presents. Contrary to the rules of science, instead of testing hypotheses by trying to prove them wrong, people will seek data that is compatible with their current beliefs.

The tendency to like or dislike everything about a person, even things not observed, is known as the halo effect. The sequence in which we see the characteristics of a person is determined by chance. Sequence matters, however, because according to the halo effect, the first impression carries more weight.

System 1 is very good at building the best possible interpretation with the ideas that are available, but it does not consider ideas that it does not have. WYSIATI, "what you see is all there is," explains how System 1 jumps to conclusions on the basis of limited evidence in intuitive thinking. WYSIATI explains several biases and judgments of choice. Overconfidence, where the brain fails to realize that evidence is missing, is on this list. Another on the list is framing effects where different ways of presenting the same information evoke different emotions. Base-rate neglect, where statistical facts are ignored, is a third type of error on this list.

Key Takeaways

- System 1 functions mainly by jumping to conclusions based on experience.

- The halo effect occurs when someone has the tendency to like or dislike everything about another person based on first impressions.

- WYSIATI or "what you see is all there is" explains how System 1 jumps to conclusions on the basis of limited evidence.

Chapter 8

Questions from System 1 are directed to System 2, which will search the brain's memory to find the answers. System 1 continuously monitors what is going on outside and inside the mind. Evaluating people as attractive or unattractive is a basic assessment. It happens automatically, whether a person wants it to or not, and it influences that person. Alex Todorov showed that people have the ability to evaluate the shape of a stranger's face to determine how dominant he is and how trustworthy he is. This survival mechanism of the brain comes into play in modern times when, for example, choosing a candidate in an election.

System 1 provides an underlying scale of intensity which allows matching across diverse dimensions. For example, if crimes were colors, murder would be a deeper shade of red than theft. This process is called intensity matching.

Another aspect of System 1 is the "mental shotgun" effect. It is difficult for System 1 not to do more than System 2 asks it to do. In other words, the control over retrieved ideas is not precise. System 1 often gives us more information than we want or need. This is similar to how a shotgun cannot be used to hit a particular target because a shotgun shoots pellets that scatter. With System 1, the intention to perform one computation frequently evokes another.

Key Takeaway

- Assessments made by System 1 happen automatically, use intensity matching for the sake of comparison, and are not precise. System 1 often gives more information than is wanted or needed.

Chapter 9

When a satisfactory answer to a hard question is not found, System 1 will find an easier, related question and answer it. This operation is called "substitution." In addition, the target question is the intended assessment, but the heuristic question is the easier question that is answered instead. Heuristics (rules of thumb) are the result of the mental shotgun, the imprecise control people have over targeting the responses to questions. Retrieving an answer from a heuristic question is often followed by an intensity match to further hone the answer to the question. A lazy System 2 often endorses a heuristic answer without checking to see if it is appropriate.

Psychologist Paul Slovic has proposed that there is an affect heuristic in which people let their likes and dislikes determine their beliefs about the world. System 2 is set up for self-criticism, but its search for information and arguments is mostly constrained to information that is consistent with existing beliefs.

Key Takeaways

- Substitution occurs when System 1 cannot find a quick answer to a hard question. It will instead find an easier, related question and answer it.

- System 2 is designed to be lazy, and it usually searches for information that is consistent with existing beliefs.

Part 2

Chapter 10

People have wrong intuitions and a poor understanding of sampling effects as a result of the way System 1 works. People are prone to exaggerate the coherence and consistency of what they see. Researchers also have shown an unsupported faith in what can be learned from a few observations, even though it is widely known that large samples are more precise than small samples. Our preference for causal thinking leads us to make serious mistakes when evaluating the randomness of truly random events. Our downfall occurs because we are pattern seekers and believers in a coherent world. People pay more attention to the content of messages than to reliability of the information. Causal explanations of chance events are generally wrong.

Key Takeaway

- System 1 is constantly searching for causal explanations in an effort to make situations appear coherent and consistent. These explanations are often wrong because they are based on small samples instead of large ones.

Chapter 11

The anchoring effect is a phenomenon that occurs when people consider a particular value for an unknown quantity before estimating that quantity. The estimates stay close to the number that was considered, hence the image of an anchor. For example, if a person considers how much should be paid when buying a house, that person will be influenced by the asking price of the house. The asking price becomes the anchor for the estimated value. Adjustment is a deliberate attempt to find reasons to move away from the anchor. Research has confirmed that adjustment involves effort. People adjust less (stay closer to the anchor) when their mental resources are depleted. Anchoring effects, sometimes due to priming and sometimes due to insufficient adjustment, are everywhere. The psychological processes that produce anchoring make us far more suggestible than we want to be.

Key Takeaway

- The anchoring effect occurs when people consider a certain value for an unknown quantity before estimating what they think the quantity ought to be.

Chapter 12

When people want to estimate the frequency of a category, the availability heuristic is what occurs. Instances of a class are retrieved from memory. If retrieval is easy and fluent, the category will be judged to be large. It was shown that both System 1 and System 2 are involved in this process. Factors that are a potential source of bias when estimating the frequency of a category include: an important event that attracts attention, a dramatic event, and personal experiences. Studies led by psychologist Norbert Schwarz observed that the task of listing instances may enhance the judgments of the trait in two ways: by the number of instances retrieved and the ease with which they come to mind.

Key Takeaway

- The availability heuristic occurs when an estimate for the frequency of a category is influenced by the number of instances retrieved from memory and how easily they come to mind.

Chapter 13

Peoples' expectations about the frequency of events are distorted by the prevalence and emotional intensity of the media coverage to which they are exposed. The mechanism through which biases are changed into policy is called the availability cascade. Availability provides a heuristic for judgments other than frequency. Specifically, the importance of an idea is often judged by the emotional charge and ease with which the idea comes to mind. An availability cascade is a self-sustaining chain of events, which may start from media reports of a relatively minor event and lead up to public panic and large-scale government action.

It has been found that people have a basic limitation in the ability of their minds to deal with small risks. They either ignore them altogether or give them too much weight, with nothing in between.

Key Takeaways

- An availability cascade happens when a minor event is inflated by the media creating biases in peoples' minds, and these biases are changed into policy.

- When dealing with small risks, people generally either ignore them altogether or give them too much credence.

Chapter 14

Base rate in statistics is the average number of times an event occurs divided by the average number of times on which it might occur. Representativeness is when people focus exclusively on stereotypes and ignore both the base rate and any doubts they have about the truth of the stereotype. The puzzle called "Tom W's Specialty" helped show how people use base rate and representativeness to determine what they thought Tom W's college specialty was. They based their answers on representativeness and ignored the base rate. Judging probability by representativeness does have a positive aspect: the intuitive impressions that it creates are often more accurate than chance guesses would be.

Bayesian reasoning can be summarized in two simple statements: anchoring judgment of the probability of an outcome on a plausible base rate and questioning the diagnostic validity of the evidence.

Key Takeaway

- Representativeness is the exclusive focus on stereotypes, ignoring both the base rate and any doubts about the truth of the stereotype.

Chapter 15

Kahneman and Tvresky created the "Linda problem" hoping to provide conclusive evidence of the role of heuristics in judgment and of their incompatibility with logic. Participants in the study were given a description of an imaginary person named Linda. They were then given a list of possible scenarios for Linda and asked to rank them according to the likelihood of them being true based on the description they had been given. Linda is described as being concerned with discrimination. One possible choice in the ranking list was that Linda is a bank teller. Another choice was that Linda is a bank teller and is active in the feminist movement. Participants in the study ranked the option which included feminist movement as a higher probability than the option that did not include it. Logically, the set of bank tellers is larger than, and includes, the set of bank tellers who are active in the feminist movement. Therefore, the logical choice should have been to rank the option of bank tellers that did not include feminist movement higher than the one that did include it. When logic was pitted against representativeness (stereotypes), representativeness won out. This showed a failure on the part of System 2.

The word fallacy is used when people fail to apply a logical rule that is obviously relevant. The Linda study introduced the idea of a conjunction fallacy, which people commit when they judge a conjunction of two events to be more probable than one of the events in a direct comparison. It was also suggested that the ideas of coherence, plausibility, and probability are easily confused. Joint evaluation allows a comparison of two sets, while single evaluation shows only one of the two sets. Sometimes a less-is-more pattern emerges because System 1 averages instead of adding. This is what happened in the Linda problem. Although the choice of "Linda is a feminist bank teller" is smaller than and is a subset of the larger set of "Linda is a bank teller," participants viewed it as being more probable.

Key Takeaways

- Making judgments based on stereotypes wins out over judgments based on logic. This is a failure of System 2.

- People commit a conjunction fallacy when they judge a conjunction of two events to be more probable than one of the events in a direct comparison.

- Because System 1 averages instead of adding, a less-is-more pattern sometimes emerges.

Chapter 16

Statistical base rates are facts about a population but are not relevant to the individual case. Causal base rates change a person's view of how the individual case came to be. Stereotypes are statements about the group that are accepted as facts about every member. Stereotyping has a bad connotation in our culture, but when used in psychological testing, it has a neutral meaning. One of the basic characteristics of System 1 is that it represents categories as norms. When categories are social, the representations are called stereotypes. Hostile stereotyping in society is wrong and can have dreadful consequences.

Psychologically, however, the fact cannot be avoided that stereotypes are how we think of categories.

Teaching psychology is basically a waste of time because people will not draw from base-rate information an inference that conflicts with other beliefs. When people are taught surprising statistical facts about human behavior, their understanding of the world has not really changed. There is a deep gap between how people think about statistics and how they think about individual cases. When statistical results have a causal interpretation, people are more likely to believe them than if they are based on non-causal information. However, even compelling causal information will not change long-held beliefs or beliefs rooted in personal experience.

Key Takeaways

- People think of categories in stereotypes and believe causal information over non-causal information.

- Compelling causal information will not change long-held beliefs or beliefs rooted in personal experience.

Chapter 17

Regression to the mean is a statistical term describing the phenomenon that if a variable is extreme on its first measurement, it will tend to be closer to the average on its second measurement. Additionally, if it is extreme on its second measurement, it will tend to have been closer to the average on its first. In other words, it is the inevitable fluctuation of a random process. The mind is strongly biased toward causal explanations and does not deal well with statistics. Furthermore, causal explanations will be evoked when regression is detected, but they will be wrong because the truth is that regression to the mean has an explanation but does not have a cause.

Key Takeaways

- Regression to the mean is a statistical term describing the inevitable fluctuation of a random process.

- When the mind detects regression, it wrongly evokes a causal explanation.

Instaread on Thinking, Fast and Slow by Daniel Kahneman

Chapter 18

There are many occasions in life when predictions need to be made. People are often asked for a prediction, but they substitute an evaluation of the evidence, not noticing that the question they answer is not the one that was asked. Their predictions, then, are systematically biased. They ignore the regression to the mean. Correcting intuitive predictions is a task for System 2. Much effort is required to find the relevant reference category, estimate the baseline prediction, and evaluate the quality of the evidence. The intuitions of System 1 deliver predictions that are too extreme, and people put too much faith in them. Regression is a problem for System 2, as well, because the idea of the regression to the mean is foreign and difficult to communicate and comprehend.

Key Takeaway

- System 1 delivers intuitive predictions that are too extreme and must be corrected by System 2. Correcting these predictions is a difficult task for System 2.

Part 3

Chapter 19

Psychologist and statistician, Nassim Taleb, introduced the idea of a narrative fallacy which describes how flawed stories of the past shape our views of the world and our expectations for the future. Narrative fallacies arise from our continuous attempt to make sense of the world. In these fallacies, people tend to exaggerate the role of skill and underestimate the part that luck plays in the outcome. The more that luck is involved in a story, the less there is to be learned from it. The brain is a sense-making organ when it creates narratives about the past.

Hindsight bias is the inability to reconstruct past beliefs which causes people to underestimate the extent to which they are surprised by past events.

Outcome bias occurs when people blame decision-makers for good decisions that work out badly and give them too little credit for successful actions that appear obvious only after the fact. Actions that seem wise in foresight can look negligent in hindsight.

Key Takeaways

- A narrative fallacy occurs when there is confusion between the experiencing self and the remembering self. The experiencing self does the living while the remembering self keeps score and makes choices.

- Actions that seem wise in foresight can look negligent in hindsight.

Chapter 20

The illusion of validity occurs when people know as a general fact that their predictions are little better than random guesses, and yet, they feel and act as if their specific predictions are valid.

There is also an illusion of skill among people such as stock pickers. Researchers generally agree that such people are making sensible, educated guesses in a situation of great uncertainty. In these cases, educated guesses are no more accurate than blind guesses. Illusions of both validity and skill are supported by a strong professional culture. People can maintain a strong belief in any proposition when they are sustained by a community of others who are like-minded. In spite of what people may believe, reality emerges from the interactions of many forces, including luck. This often produces unpredictable outcomes.

Key Takeaways

- Illusion of validity occurs when people know their predictions are random guesses, and yet, they feel and act as if these predictions are valid.

- There is an illusion of skill in certain professions where people make educated guesses that are, in reality, no more accurate than blind guesses.

Instaread on Thinking, Fast and Slow by Daniel Kahneman

Chapter 21

In a study done by Paul Meehl, it was proved that the accuracy of experts was matched or exceeded by a simple algorithm. A classic example of a useful algorithm is the Apgar assessment score that is given to newborn babies. This systematic assessment of a newborn based on five variables has saved the lives of hundreds of thousands of infants. Newborn infants are each given a score of 0, 1, or 2 for the health of their heart rate, respiration, reflexes, muscle tone, and so on. These rating scores reveal whether the infants are in good health or are in need of immediate intervention. Before the Apgar score was used, different practitioners focused on different cues, and danger signs were often missed.

Key Takeaway

- The accuracy of simple algorithms matches or exceeds the accuracy of experts.

Chapter 22

Scholar Herbert Simon defined intuition like this: "The situation has provided a cue; this cue has given the expert access to information stored in memory, and the information provides the answer. Intuition is nothing more and nothing less than recognition." (p. 180).

Emotional learning, such as when to be afraid, is usually quick, but expertise takes a long time to develop. Expertise in a task or profession is actually a large collection of mini-skills. Two conditions must exist in order to acquire a skill: an environment that is sufficiently regular to be predictable, and an opportunity to learn these regularities through prolonged practice. Intuition cannot be trusted in the absence of stable regularities in the environment.

Key Takeaways

- Intuition is nothing more and nothing less than recognition.

- Expertise is actually a large collection of mini-skills.

Chapter 23

The inside view is the one adopted by persons working on a project to assess the future of their project. The outside view takes into account cases done by others within the same reference class. A planning fallacy occurs when plans and forecasts are made unrealistically close to best-case scenarios and could be improved by consulting the statistics of similar cases. In order to mitigate a planning fallacy, planners should make every effort to take the outside view by comparing the problem to the available relevant information from other cases. This treatment for planning fallacy is called reference class forecasting.

Key Takeaway

- A planning fallacy occurs when plans and forecasts are made unrealistically close to best-case scenarios. Planners should take the outside view to mitigate a planning fallacy.

Chapter 24

Optimistic bias occurs when people view the world as more benign than it really is, see their own attributes as more favorable than they really are, and see the goals that they adopt as more achievable than they are likely to be. Those with an optimistic bias also underestimate the odds they face and take more risks. Optimistic entrepreneurs often believe they are prudent, even when they are not, and that they are in a promising line of business, which is not always true. Optimists persist even after receiving discouraging news.

Key Takeaway

- Those with an optimistic bias underestimate the odds they face and take more risks.

Part 4

Chapter 25

Daniel Bernoulli, a Swiss mathematician and physicist, observed that most people dislike risk, and if they are offered a choice between a gamble and an amount equal to its expected value, they will choose the sure thing. Bernoulli invented psychophysics to explain this aversion to risk. He believed that people's choices are based not on dollar values but on the psychological values of outcomes, their utilities. However, later studies showed that a person's happiness is determined by the recent change in his or her wealth, relative to the different states of wealth that define his reference points. Bernoulli's model lacks the idea of a reference point.

Key Takeaways

- Daniel Bernoulli tried to explain why people have an aversion to risk, but his model lacked the idea of a reference point, so it was inaccurate.

Chapter 26

In Bernoulli's utility theory, the benefit of a gain is assessed by comparing the benefits of two states of wealth. However, Bernoulli's model has a weakness. It has a missing variable, the reference point: the earlier state relative to which gains and losses are evaluated.

Prospect theory goes beyond the utility theory. It describes how people make choices between different options or prospects when risk is involved. Prospect theory also explains how people's decisions are often based on subjective judgments instead of on objective judgments. Prospect theory is more complex than the utility theory and has three cognitive features. The first is that people make evaluations relative to a neutral reference point, usually the status quo. The second is that a principle of diminishing sensitivity applies to both sensory measurements and the evaluation of changes in wealth. For example, a weak light makes a big difference in a dark room, but the same light would be undetectable in a brightly illuminated room. In matters of wealth, people view the subjective difference between $900 and $1000 as smaller than the difference between $100 and $200. The third principle is that people are loss averse: losses loom larger than gains to them.

Key Takeaways

- The prospect theory has three cognitive features: the evaluation is relative to a neutral reference point, the principle of diminishing sensitivity applies to both sensory measurements and the evaluation of changes in wealth, and people are loss averse.

Chapter 27

The Endowment Effect occurs when an item appears to increase in value for someone who owns it. In this case, the pain of giving up something is compared to the pleasure of getting something. The main feature of the Endowment Effect is that goods for exchange are valued differently from goods to be consumed or enjoyed.

Key Takeaways

- The Endowment Effect occurs when an item appears to increase in value for someone who owns it.

- The main feature of the Endowment Effect is that goods for exchange are valued differently from goods to be consumed or enjoyed.

Chapter 28

Human brains are designed to give priority to bad news. This evolutionary history is reflected by the automatic operations of System 1. Threats are recognized and given priority over opportunities as a survival technique. Loss aversion is one of many manifestations of broad negativity dominance.

Moral rules of the public evaluate what may or may not be done concerning losses and gains. Basically, the existing wage, price, or rent sets a reference point, which has the nature of an entitlement that must not be infringed.

Key Takeaways

- Human brains are designed to give priority to bad news. Loss aversion is one manifestation of this.

- Moral rules evaluate what may or may not be done with losses and gains.

Instaread on Thinking, Fast and Slow by Daniel Kahneman

Chapter 29

When people form an evaluation of a complex object, they assign weights to its characteristics. Some characteristics influence the evaluation more than others do. The possibility effect causes highly unlikely outcomes to be weighted more than they deserve. Conversely, the certainty effect causes almost certain outcomes to be given less weight than their probability justifies. The prospect theory teaches that people attach values to gains and losses rather than to wealth, and that the decision weights that they assign to outcomes are different from probabilities. The fourfold pattern of preferences is considered one of the main achievements of prospect theory. First, people are averse to risk when they stand to achieve a substantial gain. Second, because of the possibility effect, people are indifferent to the fact that their chance of winning is very small when the top prize is very large. Third, people are willing to pay more for something than the expected value in order to eliminate a worry and to purchase peace of mind. A good example of this would be insurance. Fourth, people who face very bad options take desperate gambles with a high probability of making things worse in exchange for a small hope of avoiding a large loss.

Key Takeaway

- The fourfold pattern of preferences are as follows: people are averse to risk when they stand to achieve a substantial gain, people are indifferent to the fact that their chance of winning is very small when the top prize is very large, people are willing to pay more than the expected value in order to purchase peace of mind, and people who face bad options take desperate gambles.

Chapter 30

An availability cascade occurs when an extremely vivid image of death and damage is constantly reinforced by the media, making it highly accessible. System 1 produces an emotional response that is automatic and uncontrolled. System 2 knows that the probability of such an event is low, but it cannot turn off the response of System 1. In these cases, the actual probability does not matter. Only the possibility is of consequence. People overestimate the probability of unlikely events and give too much weight to their likelihood in their decisions. Vividness and the ease of imagining contribute to these decision weights.

Denominator neglect occurs when distinctive vividness increases the decision weight of an event. Also, denominator neglect helps explain why different ways of communicating risks vary so much in how they affect people.

Key Takeaways

- People overestimate the probability of rare events due to media reinforcement and give too much weight to their likelihood in their decisions.

- Denominator neglect occurs when distinctive vividness increases the decision weight of an event.

Chapter 31

Considering a sequence of two simple decisions separately is called narrow framing. Considering four options in a single comprehensive decision is called broad framing. Broad framing blunts the emotional reaction to losses and increases the willingness to take risks. Decision makers who are prone to narrow framing would benefit by having a risk policy that they can routinely apply whenever a relevant problem arises. Two remedies against the optimism of the planning fallacy and the caution caused by loss aversion are the outside view and the risk policy.

Key Takeaway

- Broad framing blunts the emotional reaction to losses and increases the willingness to take risks.

Chapter 32

People keep score of their actions on a scale of self-regard and achievement. These mental accounts are a form of narrow framing; they keep things under control and manageable by a finite mind.

The sunk-cost fallacy is the decision to invest additional resources in a losing account when better investments are available. People will sometimes throw good money after bad instead of accepting the humiliation of a costly failure.

Regret is an emotion and a punishment we inflict upon ourselves. The fear of regret is a factor in many of the decisions that people make. Regret is usually accompanied by feelings that one should have known better. People have a stronger emotional reaction, including regret, to an outcome produced by action than to the same outcome produced by inaction. If making a certain choice can cause harm or damage, that choice becomes a taboo trade-off because of the regret and shame it would cause. This is how moral responsibility comes into play in the choices people make.

Key Takeaways

- People keep score of their actions on a scale of self-regard and achievement.

- The sunk-cost fallacy happens when people throw good money after bad instead of accepting the humiliation of a costly failure.

- The fear of regret is a factor in many of the decisions that people make.

Chapter 33

Preference reversals come about because the beliefs that people endorse when they reflect about morality do not necessarily govern their emotional reactions. Also, the moral intuitions that come to their mind in different situations are not internally consistent. The emotional reactions of System 1 are much more likely to determine single evaluation while the comparison that occurs in joint evaluation always involves a more careful and effortful assessment, which calls for System 2.

Our world is broken into categories for which we have norms. Judgments and preferences are coherent within categories but potentially incoherent when the objects that are evaluated belong to different categories.

Key Takeaway

- Preference reversals occur because the beliefs that people endorse when they reflect about morality do not necessarily govern their emotional reactions.

Chapter 34

Some meanings are reality bound while other meanings relate to what happens to a person's System 1 as he understands it. The fact that logically equivalent statements evoke different reactions when they are framed emotionally makes it impossible for humans to be reliably rational. Choices are not reality-bound because System 1 is not reality-bound. Moral feelings are attached to frames, descriptions of reality, rather than to reality itself.

Key Takeaways

- The fact that logically equal statements cause different reactions when they are framed emotionally makes it impossible for humans to be reliably rational.

Part 5

Chapter 35

Mentally, people have two selves, their experiencing-self and their remembering-self. The experiencing-self answers the question, "How are things right now?" The remembering-self answers the question, "How was it, on the whole?" Memories are all we get to keep from our experience of living. Confusing experience with the memory of it is a compelling cognitive illusion.

Key Takeaways

- People have two mental selves, their experiencing-self and their remembering-self.

Chapter 36

The remembering-self works by composing stories and keeping them for future reference. Everyone cares intensely about the narrative of his or her own life and wants it to be a good story. In the intuitive evaluation of whole lives, as well as in small parts of them, peaks and ends matter but duration does not.

Key Takeaways

- The remembering-self works by creating stories and keeping them for future reference.

Chapter 37

Experienced well-being occurs when people's lives are filled with experiences they would rather continue than stop. Total absorption in a task, known as flow, is an indication of having a good time. Resistance to interruption is a sign that someone is experiencing well-being. The percentage of time that an individual spends in an unpleasant state is known as the U-index. Basically, there are two aspects of well-being. The first is the well-being that people experience as they live their lives. The second is the judgment they make when they evaluate their lives. When considering the question of whether or not money can buy happiness, the conclusion can be drawn that being poor makes a person miserable and that being rich may enhance a person's life satisfaction but does not generally improve experienced well-being. The easiest way for people to increase happiness is to control their use of time. Finding more time to do the things they enjoy will increase their happiness level.

Key Takeaway

- Experienced well-being occurs when people's lives are filled with experiences they would rather continue than stop. Resistance to interruption is a sign that someone is experiencing well-being.

Chapter 38

When thinking about life and how satisfied people are with their lives, several conclusions can be made. Affective forecasting occurs when people are aware of certain statistics concerning a decision they are making, but they do not believe these statistics apply to them. The focusing illusion can be described in this way: "Nothing in life is as important as you think it is when you are thinking about it." (p. 305). In other words, the focusing illusion exaggerates the importance of some aspect or element of a situation. Over time, attention is withdrawn from a new situation as it becomes more familiar. The mind is good with stories, but it is not well designed for the processing of time.

Key Takeaways

- Affective forecasting, the focusing illusion, and the passing of time all influence how satisfied people are with their lives.

- The mind is good with stories, but it is not well designed for the processing of time.

Conclusions

The discussion in this book is centered on three different pairs. The first discussion is about the characteristics and qualities of the two systems of the brain: System 1, which does the fast thinking, and System 2, which does the slow thinking. The two species are the next pair. This discussion compares those who live in the land of theory, Econs, with those who act in the real world, Humans. The third pair set up for comparison is the experiencing-self and the remembering-self. The experiencing-self does the living while the remembering-self keeps score and makes choices.

A Reader's Perspective

Thinking, Fast and Slow by Daniel Kahneman is a comprehensive look at the way our brains try to make sense of the world around us through both our innate intuitions and our deliberate thoughts. Kahneman sets out to explore and explain the many errors we have in judgment. Based on decades of psychological and statistical research, Kahneman describes how and why our mental fallacies come about by providing a new vocabulary of defining terms that relate to this subject.

In an attempt to reach the lay reader, Kahneman sets up the fictional characters of his book as System 1 and System 2 to refer to the automatic, intuitive side of the brain as opposed to the deliberate, thinking side of the brain. This tactic seems condescending and annoying instead of being clarifying and engaging as the author intended. Each of the systems, which the author readily admits do not even physically exist, has its own personality, attributes, characteristics, and duties. This attempt at simplifying how we look at the brain at the beginning of the book seems odd and contrived, especially when later the book becomes quite tedious and scholarly, bogged down by a hodgepodge of unconnected and complicated mathematical and statistical examples and graphs. It is contradictory to create oversimplified puppet-like fictional characters out of functions of the brain to make the concepts easier to understand and then create a whole new vocabulary of pedantic, erudite, unnecessary terms and definitions to describe the subject. If this book is intended to capture the interest and attention of the lay reader, it fails miserably.

Instaread on Thinking, Fast and Slow by Daniel Kahneman

Much of the book is devoted to listing the findings of researchers who have studied different aspects of the rational brain versus the irrational brain. These examples are random and unconnected to each other making the book feel choppy and abrupt. The flow of the book is also interrupted by formatting errors which jolt and distract the reader from the content of the book. Although Kahneman begins the book by saying he will be comparing System 1 and System 2 as processes of the brain, he then switches in the middle of the book to talking about two species, those who live in the land of theory and those who act in the real world. He switches topics once again at the end of the book to talk about the experiencing-self and the remembering-self. This switching of topics detracts from the author's whole underlying theme of using System 1 and System 2 as fictional characters in the book because the characters are basically abandoned as he moves on to other parts of the book.

Kahneman's research is well-documented, and I have no doubt that he invested a great deal of time in studying and learning about the topic of mental fallacies in order to write about it. He obviously has a love of the subject as he describes the hours he spent learning about it with his research partner. However, by trying to reach both the lay reader and the scholarly researcher, he fails both groups. Kahneman made some interesting points, but they got lost in the language he used. Scholarly readers and perhaps, lay readers as well, will most likely be put off by the condescending creation of the fictional characters System 1 and System 2. The author hopes that lay readers will talk about his new terms and definitions around the office water cooler and use these terms to help them realize and discuss the errors in their thinking. Most likely, the readers will get about a third of the way into the book, be bored with it, and stop reading it. They will realize the mental error they made was in purchasing this tedious book in the first place.

~~~~ END OF INSTAREAD ~~~~

Instaread on Thinking, Fast and Slow by Daniel Kahneman

Thank you for purchasing this Instaread book

Download the Instaread mobile app to get unlimited text & audio summaries of bestselling books.

Visit Instaread.co to learn more.